Living and Nonliving in the

Grasslands

Rebecca Rissman

Raintree

Raintree is an imprint of Capstone Global Library Limited, a company incorporated in England and Wales having its registered office at 7 Pilgrim Street, London, EC4V 6LB – Registered company number: 6695582

www.raintreepublishers.co.uk
myorders@raintreepublishers.co.uk

Edited by Daniel Nunn, Rebecca Rissman, and Catherine Veitch
Designed by Cynthia Della-Rovere
Picture research by Tracy Cummins
Production by Sophia Argyris
Originated by Capstone Global Library Ltd
Printed and bound in China by Leo Paper Products Ltd

ISBN 978 1 406 26592 7 (hardback)
17 16 15 14 13
10 9 8 7 6 5 4 3 2 1

ISBN 978 1 406 26599 6 (paperback)
18 17 16 15 14
10 9 8 7 6 5 4 3 2 1

British Library Cataloguing in Publication Data
A full catalogue record for this book is available from the British Library.

Acknowledgements
We would like to thank the following for permission to reproduce photographs: istockphoto pp. 9 (© Richard Gillard), 22 (© Justin Matley); Shutterstock pp. 1, 19 (© Maksym Protsenko), 4, 23b (© Vadim Petrakov), 5 (© l i g h t p o e t), 6, 23d (© Galyna Andrushko), 7 (© Amelandfoto), 8, 23c (© Pavelk), 10 (© Jason Prince), 11 (© Dave Pusey), 12 (© Anna Diederich), 14 (© Simon_g), 15 (© Tony Campbell), 16 (© Sinelyov), 18 (© Mazzzur), 20, 23a (© Slawek Kuter), 21 (© Alta Oosthuizen); Superstock pp. 13 (Peter Blahut / All Canada Photos), 17 (Cusp).

Front cover photograph of African elephant reproduced with permission of Superstock (© Corbis).

We would like to thank Michael Bright and Diana Bentley for their invaluable help in the preparation of this book.

Every effort has been made to contact copyright holders of material reproduced in this book. Any omissions will be rectified in subsequent printings if notice is given to the publisher.

All the Internet addresses (URLs) given in this book were valid at the time of going to press. However, due to the dynamic nature of the Internet, some addresses may have changed, or sites may have changed or ceased to exist since publication. While the author and publisher regret any inconvenience this may cause readers, no responsibility for any such changes can be accepted by either the author or the publisher.

Some words are in bold, **like this**.
You can find them in the glossary on page 23.

Contents

What is a grassland?

A grassland is a large area of land covered in grasses.
Grasslands have few trees.

Different types of plants and animals live in grasslands.
There are **non-living** things in grasslands, too.

What are living things?

Living things are alive. Living things need air and **sunlight**. Living things move on their own.

Living things grow and change.

Living things need food and water.

What are non-living things?

Non-living things are not alive. Non-living things do not need air and **sunlight**.

Non-living things do not need food or water.

non-living

Non-living things do not grow and change on their own.
Non-living things do not move on their own.

Is a lion living or non-living?

A lion needs food and water.

A lion moves on its own.

A lion grows and changes.

A lion needs air and **sunlight**.

A lion is **living**.

Is a rock living or non-living?

A rock does not move on its own.

A rock does not grow and change on its own.

A rock does not need food or water.

A rock does not need air or **sunlight**.

A rock is **non-living**.

Is a bird living or non-living?

A bird grows and changes.

A bird moves on its own.

A bird needs food and water.

A bird needs air and **sunlight**.

A bird is **living**.

Is soil living or non-living?

Soil does not move on its own.

Soil does not need food or water.

Soil does not grow and change on its own.

Soil does not need air and **sunlight**.

Soil is **non-living**.

Is grass living or non-living?

Grass grows and changes.

Grass needs water.

Grass moves on its own towards the sun.

Grass needs air and **sunlight**.

Grass is **living**.

Is a grasshopper living or non-living?

A **grasshopper** moves on its own.

A grasshopper needs food and water.

A grasshopper grows and changes.

A grasshopper needs air and **sunlight**.

A grasshopper is **living**.

What do you think?

Is this stream **living** or **non-living**?

Glossary

grasshopper type of insect that can jump very high

living alive. Living things need food and water. They breathe and move on their own. They grow and change.

non-living not alive. Non-living things do not need food or water. They do not move on their own. They do not grow and change on their own.

sunlight light from the sun

Find out more

Websites

Click through these images of living and non-living things, then take a quiz!
www.bbc.co.uk/schools/scienceclips/ages/5_6/ourselves.shtml

Check out this site to learn more about what living things need.
www.kidsbiology.com/biology_basics/needs_living_things/living_things_have_needs1.php

Go to this site and try to spot all the living things in the park!
www.sciencekids.co.nz/gamesactivities/plantsanimals.html

Books

A Grassland Habitat (Introducing Habitats), Kelley MacAulay and Bobbie Kalman (Crabtree, 2006)

Animal Babies in Grasslands, Jennifer Schofield (Kingfisher, 2004)

Living and Nonliving, Carol K. Lindeen (Capstone Press, 2008)

Index